D1500159

Daniel on Solid Ground

Arthur J. Ferch

Review and Herald Publishing Association
Washington, DC 20039-0555
Hagerstown, MD 21740

The author assumes full responsibility for the accuracy
of all facts and quotations cited in this book.

This book was
Edited by Richard W. Coffen
Designed by Dennis Ferree
Cover design by Bill Kirstein
Cover illustration by Jerry Dadds
Type set: Times Roman

Texts credited to NIV are from the *Holy Bible, New International
Version*. Copyright © 1973, 1978, International Bible Society. Used by
permission of Zondervan Bible Publishers.

PRINTED IN U.S.A.

Library of Congress Cataloging in Publication Data

Ferch, Arthur J., 1940-
  Daniel on solid ground.

  Includes bibliographies.
  1. Bible. O.T. Daniel—Criticism, interpretation, etc. I. Title.

BS1555.2.F47 1988   224'.506   88-1959
ISBN 0-8280-0427-7

CONTENTS

Dedicated

to my students,
from whom I learned much.

Preface

The book of Daniel is remarkably similar to, yet significantly different from, many of the other biblical documents. Like the books of Joshua, Judges, Samuel, and Kings, Daniel consists of historical narratives (Dan. 1; 3-6). Yet unlike the historical books, more than half of this slender volume consists of prophecies regarding the future (Dan. 2; 7-12). English Bibles include the book of Daniel among the prophets. However, while the prophets frequently claim that the "word of the Lord" came to them directly (e.g., Joel 1:1; Micah 1:1; Zeph. 1:1, etc.), a heavenly bystander interprets Daniel's visions and dreams to the seer (e.g., Dan. 7:16, 23; 8:15, 16, 19; 9:21; 10:10, 11).

Daniel belonged to the class of wise men (Dan. 1:17-20; 2:12-27, 48; 5:10-12); nevertheless, his counsels read differently from those in the books of Proverbs, Job, or Ecclesiastes. Because the book of Daniel resembles most closely that of Revelation (which in Greek is called *Apocalypse*), it is often grouped with other apocalyptic documents, be they biblical or extrabiblical. Yet it is unique even among these writings. In common with most Old Testament writers, Daniel reveals a particular interest in the welfare of Jerusalem and Israel. However, unlike other biblical authors, he concentrates on the Gentile nations and their place within the larger plan and purpose of God.

This short biblical work has been subjected to intense debate and varied interpretations, particularly during the past 150 years. Positions on which both Jews and Christians had generally agreed for centuries are now challenged by biblical scholars. Significant in this shift are questions of presuppositions and introduction, specifically issues dealing with the text, authorship, unity, date, nature, and interpretation of the book of Daniel.

The aim of this monograph is twofold. First, it is to acquaint readers with several of the issues that have contributed to the radical change in our modern understanding of the book of Daniel. Second, it is to review critically some of the reasons historico-critical scholars have advanced in support of the shift in understanding. To this end, the volume will reflect largely on the scholarly discussion of the past two decades. This book, then, is neither a commentary nor a homily, but an introduction seeking to address the issues of text, canon, authorship, unity, date, alleged resemblances between the second century B.C. in Judea and in Daniel, apocalyptic, and historicism. Our assessment of these questions determines our whole approach to the book of Daniel.

In order to make this volume accessible to a wide readership, I have endeavored to minimize both technical discussion and the use of foreign words, providing both transliteration and translation. I have used the word *Daniel* to refer both to the author and to the book as a whole. The context will clarify the particular use made. I have used primarily the New International Version of the Bible or given my own translation of the biblical text.

I would like to register my gratitude to the Avondale College Foundation for its research grant so willingly provided. Thanks are due also to my family for their patience and to Miss Carolyn Campbell for her assistance with the typing of the manuscript.

It is my prayer that this volume may deepen the reader's confidence in God's control of and purpose for the whole of history.

CHAPTER ONE

Text and Canon

N o other book of the Bible is as puzzling as is the book of Daniel when it comes to both the place it occupies in the sacred canon and its length. Various language editions assign different places to Daniel within the order of Old Testament books. Furthermore, some translations (or versions, as they are also known) contain a shorter and others a much longer text of the book of Daniel. This chapter discusses the place of the book of Daniel in the canon, or collection of Old Testament books, and reviews the differences in the actual length of the text. These differences of both the placement and the size of the book have led some modern biblical scholars to the conclusion that the book of Daniel should not be included among the section of the Prophets and that it received its final form much later than the book itself claims.

The Old Testament has been customarily divided into three sections, designated as the *Law* (the first five books of the Bible), the *Prophets* (which include Joshua, Judges, Samuel, and Kings, as well as Isaiah, Jeremiah, Ezekiel, and the 12 minor prophets, Hosea-Malachi), and the *Writings* (consisting of the remainder of the Old Testament books). This tripartite division was already in vogue in the time of Jesus. Appearing to the disciples after His resurrection, Jesus said to them, "Everything must be fulfilled that is written about me in the Law of Moses, the Prophets and the Psalms [as the Writings were customarily referred to]" (Luke 24:44, NIV). According to Scripture itself, the Books of the Law were penned first, the Prophets followed, and some of the books now included among the Writings (e.g., Chronicles, Ezra, Nehemiah) were placed toward the end of the Old Testament canon (see Matt. 23:35).

Whereas ancient translations and modern Christian editions of the Bible place the book of Daniel among the Prophets (generally after Ezekiel), the Hebrew Bible represented by the Masoretic or traditional text established by Jewish scholars between the sixth and ninth centuries A.D. listed it among the Writings (generally before Ezra). This order in the Masoretic Bible has led scholars to suggest that the book of Daniel as a whole was not as ancient as the Prophets, but originated well after the collection of prophetic books had closed. Such a claim, however, contravenes the book's own testimony.

The place of Daniel among the Prophets is ancient. Already in pre-Christian times, circles like those on the western shores of the Dead Sea considered Daniel to be a prophet. This is evident from fragments of an eschatological text (technically known as 4QFlor) which employs quotations from Daniel 12:10 and 11:32 that are introduced with the words "written in the book of the prophet Daniel." Obviously the community of Jews living at Qumran at the turn of the era considered Daniel to have been a prophet.

Greek translations of the Old Testament, such as the Septuagint (commonly known by the symbol LXX) and "Theodotion" (see below), both dating to pre-New Testament times, place the book of Daniel in the second division of the Old Testament known as the Prophets.

In the only direct and explicit reference to the person of Daniel in the New Testament, Jesus designated him a prophet when He said, "So when you see standing in the holy place 'the abomination that causes desolation,' spoken of through the prophet Daniel—let the reader understand—then let those who are in Judea flee to the mountains" (Matt. 24:15, 16, NIV). The Jewish historian Josephus (c. A.D. 37-c. A.D. 100) likewise spoke of Daniel as "one of the greatest of the prophets."

We are not certain why the Masoretic text placed the book of Daniel among the Writings, before the book of Ezra. However, the suggestion that Ezra and Daniel were put next to each other because they were written in a mixture of Hebrew and Aramaic deserves serious consideration. Another conjecture, not without merit, is that the rabbis omitted Daniel from the Prophets because Daniel was first and foremost a statesman rather than a member of the prophetic order.

Clearly, the later post-New Testament order of Old Testament books advanced by the rabbis does not substantiate the modern notion that the book of Daniel originated much later than the book itself claims. In sum, the evidence from the Dead Sea scrolls, the LXX, "Theodotion," Jesus, and Josephus—all of which precede the testimony of the Masoretic text—assures Daniel a place among the Prophets.

We have already mentioned the shorter and longer editions of the book of Daniel. The shorter version of the book is found in modern English Bibles, which divide the book into 12 chapters with 357 verses. Except for some minor and inconsequential changes in verse divisions, the shorter edition and its order were inherited from Jewish tradition as represented in the Masoretic text.

The Masoretic or traditional text is generally reflected in older text fragments that go back to the first and/or second centuries B.C. Among the documents discovered after World War II in caves on the western shore of the Dead Sea were some 10 fragments of

Daniel. Apart from minor differences in spelling and writing, these coincide with the much later text of the Masoretes and support the shorter editions of the text of Daniel both in content and length.

Both the Dead Sea scrolls and the Masoretic text testify that the book of Daniel was originally written in Hebrew and Aramaic. The Hebrew and Aramaic portions of Daniel were translated into Greek several centuries after their original composition. Actually, two early distinct and rival Greek translations of the book of Daniel were produced and used. These are known as the LXX and the version of Theodotion.

The LXX is a pre-Christian version that came into wide use in the first century B.C. in the city of Alexandria in Egypt with the Greek translation of the Pentateuch. According to tradition, this first section of the LXX goes back to the third century B.C. The Church Father Jerome (c. A.D. 324-420) claimed that the early Christian church rejected the LXX version of Daniel and preferred the translation of Theodotion. Nevertheless, some use was made of both, as is evident from the New Testament.

The precise date and place of origin of the Theodotionic version are still debated. However, it is now clear to scholars that the ancient tradition, which attributed this translation to Theodotion, a pious Jew of the second century A.D., must be revised. Scholars assure us that we must now assume a much earlier date for this translation. The evidence for this revised view is found in the fact that the New Testament writers had already utilized the version of Daniel in "Theodotion." For example, the book of Revelation cites readings from Daniel 7:13 that follow the translations of the LXX and "Theodotion." Thus Revelation 1:7, speaking of the second coming of Christ, gives the reading "Behold he comes *with* clouds," which represents the Theodotionic translation of Daniel 7:13. On the other hand, Revelation 14:14, following the LXX translation, describes the return of the One like the Son of man as occurring "*upon* the cloud." Given this and other citations in the New Testament of readings from "Theodotion," we must now postulate that the Theodotionic version of Daniel came into existence at least a century earlier than previously assumed. With this in mind, we will use the convention "Theodotion" when referring to this second Greek rendition of the book of Daniel.

While the "Theodotion" version of Daniel corresponds rather closely with the original Hebrew and Aramaic portions of Daniel, the LXX translation tends to be loose, particularly when one compares Daniel 3-6 in the two versions.

A more specific example, taken from the visions of Daniel, that illustrates this freedom is the LXX rendition of Daniel 7:13. In translation it reads "And behold upon the clouds of heaven came one like the Son of man *as* an Ancient of Days." Evidently, the LXX translation identifies the Ancient of Days with the "one like the son of man"; whereas "Theodotion," like the Aramaic original from which it was derived, distinguishes between these two figures.

Though the precise reason for early Christian preference for the "Theodotion" translation of Daniel remains unclear, scholars have conjectured that it may rest on the much closer similarity between its Greek rendition and the Hebrew and Aramaic originals.

Both the LXX and "Theodotion" (as well as the much later translation of Daniel into Latin called the Vulgate and produced by Jerome between A.D. 389-392) include in their text material that virtually doubles the content of the shorter text found in the Hebrew edition and in modern Protestant versions.

Inserted between Daniel 3:23 and 24 are 67 verses that report the "Prayer of Azariah" and the "Song of the Three Young Men," extending the chapter from 30 to 97 verses.

The "Prayer of Azariah" reports the confession and prayer for deliverance offered by Azariah in the fiery oven. The section concludes by noting that the descent of the Lord's angel into the furnace caused a pleasant wind to blow on the three worthies.

The "Song of the Three Young Men" is a hymn of praise offered by Hananiah, Mishael, and Azariah in the furnace in which they call upon all creation to ascribe blessing unto the Lord.

The Greek versions also append two additional chapters. The first is entitled "Susanna and the Elders" (Dan. 13), and the second is known as "Bel and the Dragon" (Dan. 14).

The former records the defamation of a beautiful and virtuous woman by two wicked and lecherous Jewish elders. The woman, whose name is Susanna, is saved from sure death by Daniel's intervention.

"Bel and the Dragon" magnifies Daniel's wisdom, prowess, and faith by reporting his exposure of the priests of Bel, his defeat of a dragon, and his deliverance from another lions' den.

Roman Catholics, in harmony with the decisions of the Council of Trent (A.D. 1545-1563), accept these additions as inspired and consider them to be deuterocanonical (that is, a secondary addition to the canon). Protestant and Jewish Bibles, on the other hand, regard these portions as apocryphal and exclude them from the sacred canon.

Most recently, historicocritical scholars have suggested that these apocryphal additions represent one of the latest stages in the book's development. However, there is no demonstrable evidence to warrant such a theory.

While some Jews included these sections when they translated the book of Daniel into Greek, several reasons support their exclusion from the canon. First, there is no trace of the apocryphal sections in the Dead Sea scrolls of Daniel discovered thus far. Second, the New Testament writers do not cite any of these sources. Third, the much later Jewish tradition, reflected in the Masoretic text, rejected them. Fourth, the heightened element of the miraculous and the convoluted narrative style of the apocryphal supplements suggest that they are of a secondary nature and do not belong to the book of Daniel. Certainly, omission of the apocryphal sections in no way detracts from the message or literary style of the book; whereas their inclusion cheapens the book's ethos.

In sum, the more ancient evidence justifies the place of Daniel among the Prophets. The book's placement next to Ezra in the rabbinic writings may be explained on the basis that both Daniel and Ezra are bilingual. Furthermore, the shorter text is to be preferred in the light of the presently known Qumran material, the New Testament practice, later Jewish tradition, and the transparently secondary nature of the apocryphal additions.

However, the shorter text has come in for considerable discussion among biblical scholars who contend that it developed over the centuries in the hands of a variety of authors. It is to this subject that we turn next.

CHAPTER TWO

Authorship and Unity

Introduction

Literary analysis (often called literary criticism) has as its domain any written document. Because the book of Daniel is a literary work, it remains open to literary analysis, as do all the books of the Bible. During the past two decades a great deal of printer's ink has been spilled on the issue. In this chapter we propose to review briefly some of the major arguments regarding both the authorship and unity of the book of Daniel.

Literary compositions differ widely, depending on authorship, purpose, nature, and time of writing. A book may be composed by one or more authors; it may be written over a short or long period of time; it may address a specific readership or a variety of audiences; it may be comprised of autobiography, history, speeches, memoirs, or other forms of material. All such factors contribute to the shape, style, structure, and interpretation of any given document. While even a single author's style may vary, depending on subject matter, audience, and time of writing, stylistic variations increase in a work composed by a number of writers.

For centuries both synagogue and church taught that the book of Daniel came from the hands of the sixth century B.C. statesman-seer known as Daniel. Apart from isolated incidents of disagreement, questions regarding authorship and literary unity were not raised until recent times.

Among those in the past who questioned the authorship were the Dutch Jewish philosopher Benedict Spinoza (A.D. 1632-1677) and the Christian English scientist Sir Isaac Newton (A.D. 1642-1727). Both Spinoza and Newton suggested that the second part of the book came from the hand of the historical Daniel but professed they had no idea as to the identity of the writer of the first half.

With the important essay of Gustav Hölscher in 1919, the debate about the unity of Daniel entered serious theological discussion.[1] Following Hölscher, an increasing number of scholars proposed numerous complex theories seeking to explain the alleged development of the book of Daniel.

After 1919 among those who still contended for the unity of Daniel was the noted English Old Testament scholar Harold H. Rowley. In his presidential address to the Society of Old Testament Study in London in January 1950, he argued arduously that an unknown author of the second century B.C. had written the entire book.

Today scholars have generally abandoned Rowley's proposal, though they agree with him that the sixth century B.C. statesman-prophet mentioned in the book was not the author. Nowadays biblical scholars generally agree (1) that several writers were responsible for the book of Daniel and (2) that the formation of the book was a long, drawn-out process which began, at the earliest, during the sixth-century B.C. Babylonian captivity and terminated in the mid-second century B.C.

The present scholarly consensus is that Daniel 7-12 arose during the religious persecutions of the Jews by the Seleucid tyrant Antiochus IV Epiphanes and were written down much later than chapters 1-6. The author or authors of chapters 7-12 incorporated into his or their work oral and/or written materials (consisting substantially of chapters 2-6) that were generated well before the time of Antiochus and for very different purposes.

Arguments Against Unity

What grounds are there for supposing that the book is a composite of several discrete documents written at different times over a period of possibly several centuries? At least three *prima facie* arguments for multiple authorship can be advanced: (1) the use of two languages—Hebrew (Dan. 1:1-2:4, first part; 8:1-12:13) and Aramaic (Dan. 2:4, last part-7:28); (2) the division of the contents into historical narratives (chapters 1, 3-6) and visions (chapters 2, 7-12); and (3) the use of third-person speech in the first half and first-person speech in the second half of the book.

Were the divisions into Hebrew and Aramaic, narratives and visions, and third- and first-person speech to occur in identical places, then of course, a strong case could be made for a variety of sources in the book of Daniel. However, all three criteria pull in different and inconclusive directions and therefore fail to demonstrate the disunity of the book.

Among other arguments advanced against the unity of Daniel are (1) alleged duplications and contradictions; (2) peculiarities of style and vocabulary; (3) apparent deficiencies in cohesion and progression between literary units; (4) differences between the Greek and Semitic texts; and (5) the implications of the modern historical analysis of Daniel.

How valid are these five arguments in favor of multiple authorship? While limits of space do not permit a detailed analysis, some brief comments need to be made before we turn to examine the evidence for the unity of the book.

Duplication of material is a well-known characteristic in Semitic documents of antiquity. One has only to turn to ancient Babylonian religious texts such as the Creation story entitled *Enuma Elish* or the Canaanite texts describing the fortunes of Baal and El to recognize the repetitious style. Yet few historians of antiquity would use the duplications in these texts as evidence for multiple authorship.

The writer of the book of Daniel was fond of lists of words. Such lists are repeated across the chapters and seem to indicate an almost unconscious stylistic penchant of the author. We read lists of words applied to the various classes of wise men, royal officers, musical instruments, and people. At any rate, arguments that insist on a particular style or vocabulary unjustifiably limit an author's freedom to vary both style and choice of words.

Some of the alleged contradictions are created by the critics. This applies particularly to the argument that chapters 1 and 2 provide two mutually exclusive depictions of Daniel. Such a contention rests purely on scholarly conjecture and need not delay us. Other possible disparities are found in the chronological data and will be discussed in greater detail in chapter three.

To cite Nebuchadnezzar's varying attitudes to Daniel's God in chapters 2 and 3 as an example for deficiency in cohesion and progression rests on the mistaken assumption that human nature is constant. Given the descriptions by Daniel of both Nebuchadnezzar and Belshazzar as fickle Eastern despots, we are hardly justified to use their changes in behavior as an argument against the literary unity of the book of

Daniel. The different faces Daniel gives to these mon-archs ring more true to life than the alleged uniformity in attitude presupposed by the critics.

Some of the differences between the Greek rendi-tions of the book of Daniel and the Masoretic text have already been touched on in the previous chapter. The question of the Greek translations is complex, and scholarly debate continues as to their origin, nature, and date. It is possible that the variations between the Semitic originals and the Greek translations result from the use of a different type of text by the translators from that represented in the Masoretic text.

Daniel 7 has suffered the greatest amount of literary dissection. The alternation between prose and poetry (evident in more modern translations), variations in introductory formulas, stylistic differences, and other criteria have led to conjectures about a complex growth of the chapter. However, many of the arguments are open to serious question.

While responsible literary analysis of the Bible is profitable, any analysis must respect first and foremost the nature of the text. In the case of chapter 7, and so much of the book as a whole, the criteria advanced in support of several textual layers reflect modern Western logic and fail to respect the ancient Eastern nature of the book. Scholars tend to judge Daniel in terms of occi-dental thought forms. Through their reconstructions of what the chapter allegedly should be like, they rob Daniel 7 of its impetus and meaning.

The most telling reason for the literary dissection of

the book, however, is not the *literary analysis* of Daniel but *historical analysis*. Historical analysts (sometimes called "critics") believe that references to the little horn in Daniel 7, 8 and to the king of the north in Daniel 11 apply to the person and work of Antiochus IV Epiphanes (175-164 B.C.). He brutally persecuted the Jews and interfered with their religious system. Consequently, modern scholars place the origin of Daniel 7-12 in the mid-second century B.C.

Since no obvious references to Antiochus and events of that period can be detected in Daniel 1-6, historians postulate a different author for the first section of Daniel. Such a procedure is dubious, for it moves from the biblical text to a conjectured historical interpretation and then imposes it upon the Scriptures. Such an approach sacrifices the primacy of the biblical text on the altar of scholarly supposition.

Indications of Unity

Most conservative Christians do not find the arguments for the composite nature of the book of Daniel compelling. However, such a negative result is in itself no proof for the unity of the work. Consequently, we must ask the question What evidence, if any, suggests a single authorship of the book?

Indications of unity, some of which Rowley suggested, include (1) the natural flow of the book in which one chapter presupposes the other; (2) themes common to both stories and visions; (3) chronological links that run across both halves of the book; (4) the interlocking of historical and prophetic chapters in Daniel 7; (5) peculiar stylistic features that are found throughout the book; (6) the progressive parallelism of the visions; and (7) the chiastic structures that tie the book together.

Chapters 1-6 are woven into one coherent unit in which successive chapters presuppose that which has gone before. Thus Daniel 2 assumes the reader's acquaintance with Nebuchadnezzar, Daniel, and his friends, all of whom had been introduced in chapter 1. Similarly, the golden image of Daniel 3, erected in honor of the king, is related to the statue of chapter 2, of which the golden head represents Nebuchadnezzar. The final events of Belshazzar's last night recorded in Daniel 5 presuppose the story of Nebuchadnezzar's madness in chapter 4 (compare Dan. 4:28-33 with 5:20, 21). The reign of Darius depicted in Daniel 6 takes for granted the fall of Babylon mentioned in Daniel 5. The narratives of Daniel set the scene and prepare the reader for the visions. The visions, on the other hand, presuppose a knowledge of Daniel the seer, the historical and geographical settings, and important aspects highlighted in the previous narratives.

Several themes are common to both halves of the book. God's unchallengeable sovereignty is repeated throughout Daniel. Passivism is enjoined upon God's people in both stories and visions. As pride precedes the fall in chapters 4 and 5, so the arrogance of the last enemy of God leads to judgment and destruction in chapters 7-12. The fulfillments of the predictions of chapters 4, 5 inspire confidence in the future fulfillments of the dreams and interpretations outlined in the visions.

The stories and visions are woven together by the chronology of Daniel's career and follow the same progress of history in parallel sequence. Thus the narratives in the first half of the book span the period of Babylon and Medo-Persia. Similarly, the visions of the second half, instead of continuing the chronological sequence from Medo-Persia onward, return to Babylon and repeat the pattern.

Daniel 7 is particularly significant because it interlocks the narratives with the prophecies by virtue of its language, symmetry, sequence, literary form, and content.

The vision of Daniel 7 is in Aramaic, as are the historical chapters. The structure of chapter 7 is an inverted parallelism (called chiasmus and discussed further below), and so are chapters 2-7 in their totality. Chapters 7-12 repeat the cycle of dates recorded in chapters 1-6, beginning with Babylon and ending with Medo-Persia. Because it contains a vision like those found in chapters 8-12, the literary form and content of Daniel 7 resembles the last five chapters of the book most closely. Yet its language and symmetry approximate the first half of the book. Daniel 7, therefore, unites the historical and visionary chapters.

Peculiar stylistic features reappear throughout the book. Thus, for example, the book speaks of several classes of wise men (Dan. 2:2, 10, 27; 4:7; 5:7, 11). Lists of royal officers (Dan. 3:2, 3; 6:7) and catalogs of instruments in Nebuchadnezzar's orchestra (Dan. 3:5, 7, 10, 15) are consistently repeated. The characteristic phrase "peoples, nations, and languages" bridges chapters 3-7. These and other features suggest the style of a single author.

Most scholars acknowledge that the visions in the book parallel each other and that later chapters progressively enlarge earlier chapters. Thus chapter 2 is the most simple; whereas the parallel chapters 7, 8-9, 10-12 increase in complexity and detail. Though the same general frame is repeated, the revelation progresses within a series of visions. It is obvious that considerable care has gone into the planning of this development.

A particular literary form known as *chiasmus* (chiasm), in which corresponding parts of a literary composition are arranged in a mirror image relationship to each other, characterizes much of Daniel. As early as 1972, A. Lenglet published an article on the literary structure of Daniel 2-7 in which he discussed the concentric symmetry of the Aramaic chapters.[2] Accordingly, the visions of chapters 2 and 7 detailing the history of empires fit like an envelope around the narratives of chapters 3-6. Chapters 3 and 6 comprise two stories of the deliverance of God's people at alternative ends of chapters 4 and 5, which both deal with God's judgment on Gentile kings. While Lenglet described this arrangement in terms of concentric circles, with one circle being contained inside the other, the literary pattern may be viewed as a chiasm:

A. *Vision* of world history (chapter 2)

  B. *Deliverance* from the fiery furnace (chapter 3)

    C. *Judgment* upon a Gentile king (chapter 4)

    C'. *Judgment* upon a Gentile king (chapter 5)

  B'. *Deliverance* from the lions' den (chapter 6)

A'. *Vision* of world history (chapter 7)

Similar chiasms occur in other chapters of the book of Daniel. Following a preliminary view of the early kingdoms (Dan. 7:2, 3), the vision of Daniel 7 flows in a sequence of units to a climax before it reverses the same thematic sequence, as the following outline illustrates:

A. First three beasts (verses 4-6)

  B. Fourth beast (verse 7)

    C. Description of the little horn speaking great things (verse 8)

      D. The Judgment (verses 9, 10 supplemented by the second half in verses 13, 14)

    C'. (Fate of) little horn speaking great things (verse 11, first part)

  B'. Fate of the fourth beast (verse 11, last part)

A'. Fate of the first three beasts (verse 12)

Other literary chiasms have been found in Daniel 8:9-12 (in terms of the horizontal and vertical activity of the little horn) and in Daniel 9:24-27, with its apex focusing on the Messiah and the provision for sin.

The linguistic structure of the book—beginning with Hebrew, passing on to Aramaic, and ending in Hebrew—also follows a chiastic pattern.

While these literary structures may not be the result of deliberate planning, they are clearly significant in any discussion of the unity of the book. Literary excisions from or dissections of the text would not only disturb the balance of the book but also would rob it of the highlights that the literary patterns suggest.

We have already observed the unique distribution of the two languages, the first- and third-person speech, and the stories and visions. When we also consider (1) the natural flow of the chapters; (2) the common themes and chronological links that run across the book; (3) the interlocking nature of Daniel 7; (4) the peculiar stylistic features found in both narratives and visions; (5) the progressive parallelisms of the visions and literary patterns that tie the book together, we have, on balance, evidence that in its totality amounts to a demonstration of the unity of the book. These indications taken together testify to a single authorship and a Semitic mind-set.

It could be argued that an editor imposed this framework upon the book as he assembled diverse materials into the one volume. Though we cannot reject such a hypothesis out of hand, the peculiar, almost

unconscious idiosyncrasies and stylistic features observed above tend to favor the notion that the book
proceeded basically from one mind and pen.

Does this evidence for unity, however, also imply
that Daniel the seer authored the book?

Authorship

We have already noted that the book is divided into
biographical (Dan. 1:1-7:2, first part; 10:1) and autobiographical sections (Dan. 7:2, last part-9:27; 10:2-
12:13). The author of at least the second half of this
work claims to have been Daniel the seer. Although it is
possible that an unknown person either wrote and/or
compiled the remaining materials, the aforementioned
distinctive arrangement, unique and virtually unconscious stylistic features, and literary patterns suggest a
single author. Juxtaposition of first- and third-person
speech was an ancient phenomenon (as any reader of
Caesar's *Gallic War* will remember) and in itself need
not mean multiple authorship. In fact, the third-person
reports of Daniel 7:1, 2 and 10:1 that begin the
autobiographic accounts of the visions interlock the
biographical and autobiographical materials, suggesting
that the author of the visions was also responsible for the
stories.

Yet a word should be added. Even if we accept
single authorship, the book obviously was not written at
a single sitting. Except for chapters 10-12, each chapter
in the book could stand by itself. Several chapters have
their own introduction and conclusion (e.g., Dan. 7:1,

28). While most chapters read like the seer's memoirs, chapter 4 is a confession of Nebuchadnezzar's, written in the form of an open letter, that Daniel apparently incorporated into his book. Most chapters are dated and specify the year during which the events recorded occurred. Though Daniel 1:7 first identifies Daniel with Belteshazzar, the correlation is repeated in Daniel 2:26; 4:8, 9, 19; 5:12; 10:1. This repetition of the name Belteshazzar, as well as that of dates, introductions, and conclusions to chapters, may indicate originally independent accounts linked by a common author.

Daniel 1 begins with events dated in the year 605 B.C. but ends by saying that Daniel's ministry would extend to the first year of Cyrus, some 70 years later (verse 21). Given the fact that the events recorded in chapters 2-5 precede the reign of Cyrus, the chronological information in Daniel 1 may suggest that the first chapter was written as an introduction to the book sometime after 539 B.C. but before chapters 10-12. According to Daniel 10:1, Daniel's last vision was given in the third year of Cyrus (i.e., 536/535 B.C.). Hence the last three chapters were penned after the rest of the book had been completed. Though the dates recorded in the chapters may not indicate the time when the individual chapters were reduced to writing, it is not impossible to speculate that the information in the chapters was recorded (at least in note form) shortly after the date specified. The seer may have kept these as a collection of memoirs.

The fact that in certain chapters Daniel uses Persian

loan words (e.g., chapters 1, 3) may further suggest that these chapters were not written before (or at least were updated by) the time that the Persian Empire succeeded the Babylonian kingdom. At that time Daniel had resumed a high administrative post and was in constant contact with his Persian colleagues. Chapters 1-9 were probably collected before the third year of Cyrus, when chapters 10-12 were added.

In sum, we may suppose that toward the end of his life Daniel, under the guidance of the Holy Spirit, drew together extracts from his memoirs and other selected materials to compile the book now known by his name. Given the argument for the unity of the book, we may further assume a unified theology rather than a combination or juxtaposition of several contesting, if not outright contradictory, theologies and messages.

The question that remains is When did Daniel compose the book bearing his name?

Present scholarship generally disputes the validity of the claims contained in the book of Daniel. How valid are the arguments advanced? Because of the crucial nature of these questions, we have devoted the following two chapters to a discussion of this issue.

References

[1]Gustav Hölscher, ''Die Entstehung des Buches Daniel,'' *Theologische Studien und Kritiken* 92 (1919) : 113-118. For a more technical discussion of the literary analysis, see Arthur J. Ferch, *The Son of Man in Daniel 7* (Berrien Springs, Mich.: Andrews University Press, 1979/1983), pp. 108-145.

[2]Ad. Lenglet, ''La structure littéraire de Daniel 2-7,'' *Biblica* 53 (1972) : 169-190.

CHAPTER THREE

The Date of Daniel

The Problems Raised by History, Language, and Extrabiblical Silence

U ntil the nineteenth century
A.D. both synagogue and church generally accepted the claims laid out in the book of Daniel. The writer of the autobiographical account (Dan. 7-12) identified himself with the Jewish protagonist described in chapters 1-6. As a young man he had been taken to Mesopotamia, where during the period of exile in Babylon (605-539 B.C.) he and several of his Hebrew friends were advanced to high administrative positions in the service of both the Neo-Babylonian and

Medo-Persian governments.

Exilic thesis—For centuries Jews and Christians believed that both the stories about Daniel and the prophecies of Daniel had their origin in the sixth and fifth centuries B.C. This conviction was based on numerous clear statements found in the book. Chapter 1 informs the reader that Daniel was captured by Nebuchadnezzar's army in the third year of the reign of King Jehoiakim (605 B.C.). The same chapter describes how Daniel rose to power and continued as a prominent political figure until the first year of King Cyrus (539 B.C.).

Other dates that may be assigned to specific chapters are the second year of Nebuchadnezzar's reign in 603 B.C. (Dan. 2:1); the first year of Belshazzar's reign in 551/550 B.C. (Dan. 7:1); the third year of Belshazzar's reign in 548/547 B.C. (Dan. 8:1); the last year of Belshazzar's reign in 539 B.C. (Dan. 5:29, 30); and the reign of Darius the Mede in 539/538 B.C. (Dan. 6:28; 9:1). The last dated revelation occurred in the third year of Cyrus' reign in 536 B.C. (Dan. 10:1).

This information is explicit and leads one to conclude that the period of Daniel's life and prophecies should be placed during the time of Judah's exile in Babylon (605 B.C. to 536 B.C.). Because of this data Klaus Koch has called this interpretation the "exilic thesis."[1] The visions in the book purport to be prophecies of events that spanned the ages from the sixth to fifth centuries B.C. to the setting up of God's kingdom; in other words, they are genuine predictions of future events (*vaticinia ante eventu,* which means "prophecies before the event").

Maccabean thesis — Since the beginning of the nineteenth century, historicocritical scholarship has challenged the exilic thesis. Following the lead of Porphyry, the third century A.D. Neoplatonist enemy of Christianity, modern scholars have assumed that the book of Daniel was composed (substantially if not entirely) during the political and religious persecutions of the Jews by the Seleucid tyrant Antiochus IV Epiphanes (175-164 B.C.). Scholars claim that the book originated in conjunction with the Jewish resistance to Antiochus led by the old Jewish priest Mattathias and his sons, known as the Maccabees.

This view, according to which the book was written *after* the crisis that it allegedly records, Koch designates the "Maccabean thesis."[2] On this interpretation the book's primary thrust deals with second century B.C. events in Jewish history and the book has no further application beyond the year 164 B.C.

It is important that we pay attention to what any book of the Bible says explicitly about its date. However, it is equally significant that we heed what the book might imply about its time of composition. Conservative scholars have customarily stressed the *explicit* testimony and thus highlighted the sixth-century date. Historicocritical scholars have been inclined to give prominence to the *implicit* data, which, they contend, argues for a second-century date. A careful appraisal of the facts must take account of *both* the explicit and implicit evidence. It must also neither suppress nor exaggerate information that may appear to either undermine or substantiate one's preferred viewpoint.

Since we have already viewed the explicit data, we will now turn to evidence that appears to suggest a later date for the book. This evidence includes (1) several alleged historical problems; (2) linguistic criteria, particularly the Persian, Greek, and Aramaic vocabulary; (3) the absence of any reference to the book in nonbiblical literature prior to 180 B.C.; and (4) the supposed close resemblances between the context of Daniel and Jewish history between 167 and 164 B.C.

In the present chapter we will examine the arguments relating to history, language, and silence regarding Daniel in contemporary external literature. The following chapter will review the fourth contention.

Alleged Historical Problems

Scholars point out certain historical problems that supposedly reveal inaccuracies. These inaccuracies, we are told, arose because the book was written centuries after the alleged events had occurred and when accurate knowledge of the facts had been lost.

The putative inaccuracies include (1) the problem of dating in Daniel 1:1; (2) the reference to Belshazzar as king; (3) the identity of Darius the Mede; and (4) the nature of the Chaldeans mentioned by Daniel as a class of professional wise men.

Date of Daniel 1:1—In his commentary on the book of Daniel, Norman Porteous claims that ''the very first statement in chapter 1 can be shown to be inaccurate.''[3] The error, according to Porteous, consists in Daniel's claim that Jehoiakim's third year coincided with Nebuchadnezzar's siege of Jerusalem. According to Porteous, the problem is further compounded by the prophet Jeremiah, who claims that Jehoiakim's fourth year concurred with Nebuchadnezzar's first year (cf. Jer. 25:1; 46:2).

It is unfortunate that despite the wealth of detailed information available about the last few decades of the state of Judah, we are still uncertain about the precise method of reckoning regnal years in southern Palestine. Two issues require consideration: (1) the beginning of the new year in Judah and (2) the use of nonaccession (antedating) and accession year (postdating) systems.

Elsewhere in the Old Testament, particularly in the historical books, where chronological discrepancies occur, harmony can be established when we assume that the civil new year in Israel generally began in the spring (in March/April—the month of Nisan), while in Judah it commenced in the autumn (in September/October—the month of Tishri). The strongest argument in favor of accepting this hypothesis regarding the beginning of the new year is that it works, thus bringing harmony to the biblical material.

It appears that in antiquity regnal years at times followed the nonaccession year principle, while on other occasions the reign of the king followed the accession year principle. According to the nonaccession year method, the portion of time between the death or deposition of a ruler and the first day of the new year was considered the *first* year of the new ruler. Thus both predecessor and successor laid claim to the same chronological period as part of their reign—for one it was his last year and for the other, his first year. Following the accession year method the first year of a king's reign was the calendar year beginning with the first day of the new year after he had ascended the throne. The days or months between the demise of the former ruler and the first day of the new year were considered the new king's accession year and reckoned as year zero.

If we assume that the author of Daniel 1:1 thought in terms of the accession year principle and began regnal years in the autumn, then the alleged historical problem is resolved. Jehoiakim's accession year would have begun right after his father Josiah died in 609 B.C., and his first year would have commenced in the fall of 608 B.C. As a result, Jehoiakim's third year extended from September/October 606 B.C. to September/October 605 B.C. Thus Nebuchadnezzar's campaign to Hattiland (which included Judah) in 605 B.C. coincided with the third year of Jehoiakim.

Further, assuming a Babylonian accession year for Nebuchadnezzar following his father's death in August 605 B.C., we can also reconcile Daniel 1:1 with Jeremiah 25:1. Jehoiakim's fourth year would have coincided with the first year of the Babylonian king either in full if Nebuchadnezzar's first year began in the autumn, or in part if following Babylonian reckoning the first year began in the spring. Rather than undermining the historical reliability of the book of Daniel, the information provided in the first verse seems to reflect a knowledge that was lost until recent times and therefore suggests a time of writing when the ancient Near Eastern methods of reckoning were still common knowledge.

King Belshazzar—Many commentators believe that the book of Daniel contains a grave historical error when it describes Belshazzar as king (Dan. 5:1, 30; 7:1; 8:1). Not one presently known Babylonian king list mentions a ruler by this name during the Neo-Babylonian period. How can this be explained?

Babylonian records reveal that Belshazzar was the eldest son of King Nabonidus and occupied the position of regent over the empire while his father was absent at Teima in Arabia. Though in Daniel's account Nebuchadnezzar is referred to as Belshazzar's father (e.g., Dan. 5:2, 11, 18), we must remember that *father* in Semitic parlance may designate no more than an ancestor or predecessor in office. Some scholars have even surmised that Belshazzar may indeed have been related to Nebuchadnezzar through his wife. However, this suggestion must remain a conjecture.

It is true that the official Babylonian records do not call Belshazzar "king," but they do state that Nabonidus "entrusted the kingship to him." The names of both Belshazzar and Nabonidus were coupled in oath formulas and in prayers on foundation documents. Clearly, then, Belshazzar received kingly dues and exercised royal prerogatives without bearing the title "king" in the Babylonian documents.

To all intents and purposes Belshazzar acted as king, and it seems a little pedantic to level the charge that the book is inaccurate because it calls him a king. In fact, according to Daniel, Belshazzar promised that the one who would read and interpret the writing on the wall would become the "third highest ruler in the kingdom" (verses 7, 16, 29). Obviously Daniel 5 reflects a state of affairs in which Belshazzar, the regent, offered Daniel a place alongside himself, the regent, and Nabonidus the king. This reveals the writer's intimate acquaintance with the contemporary situation.

Raymond Dougherty has noted: "Of all Neo-Baby-lonian records dealing with the situation at the close of the Neo-Babylonian empire, *the fifth chapter of Daniel ranks next to cuneiform literature in accuracy*, so far as outstanding events are concerned. The scriptural account may be interpreted as excelling because it employs the name Belshazzar, because it attributes royal power to Belshazzar, and because it recognizes that a dual rulership existed in the kingdom."[4]

The presentation of Belshazzar as king, rather than undermining the historicity of the book of Daniel, suggests a date well before an intimate knowledge of sixth-century conditions was lost.

Darius the Mede—The identity of Darius the Mede remains a problem. Although we cannot identify Darius with a known historical person, scholars have recommended as likely candidates the names of the Median Cyaxeres II; Ugbaru, the general who took Babylon;

Gubaru, known as governor of Babylon and the "District Beyond the River"; and Cyrus the Great.

These suggestions demonstrate that the search for the identity of the Median king is difficult but not hopeless. Given the recent findings about Belshazzar, who in former years was considered to be a fictional character, it would be unwise to dismiss as unhistorical the information Daniel provides about Darius the Mede.

The fact that Darius is referred to as king (Dan. 6:6, 12, 13) has led some writers to presume that Daniel was describing a separate Median kingdom which preceded the Neo-Babylonian empire. Others suggest that the author of Daniel confused Darius the Mede with Darius I Hystaspes (522-486 B.C.). However, such historical errors cannot be attributed to Daniel. The book clearly speaks of Medo-Persia as one empire and depicts Darius the Mede as a predecessor of Cyrus the Great and not as his successor (cf. Dan. 6:8, 12, 15, 28; 8:20).

The "Chaldeans" — *Chaldean* is used in two senses in the book of Daniel. On the one hand, it refers to the people of southern Babylonia. On the other, it is a reference to a special class of learned men. The ethnic connotation is found in Daniel 5:30, where Belshazzar is described as the king of the Chaldeans. In the same sense Darius is said to have become "king over the realm of the Chaldeans" (Dan. 9:1). This ethnic connotation continued to be used in the Old Testament and by historians as late as the Greek geographer Strabo (c. 63 B.C.-c. A.D. 24).

Elsewhere in the book of Daniel *Chaldean* has a

more restricted meaning and designates a particular class of astrologers or wise men (see Dan. 2:2, 4, 5, 10). This specialized use is also found in Herodotus (c. 484-c. 425 B.C.), where it designates priests of Bel. Scholars generally believe that this second usage of the word *Chaldean* is anachronistic.

After a thorough examination of this issue, Allan R. Millard observed that there is apparently no evidence for either use of the term *Chaldean* in Babylonian records of the sixth century B.C. The term occurs in Assyrian texts of the two previous centuries as the overall name for a group of tribes. Hence Millard concludes: "In this situation it is as improper to label the professional sense of Chaldean a sixth-century usage as it is to call it an anachronism."[5]

Linguistic Problems

Within the book of Daniel are 19 (or 20) words regarded as Persian loan words, three words considered to be of Greek origin, and six chapters that have been transmitted in the Aramaic language. Until recently critical scholars took these linguistic features as an implicit indication of a late date for the book.

Essentially the argument was that the Persian words presupposed a period of origin for the book well after the Persian empire had been established—a considerable time after 539 B.C. The Greek terms, it was argued, demand a date after the conquests of Palestine by Alexander the Great, hence after 331 B.C. The Aramaic language employed by the author appears to represent a period in the history of Aramaic found after 200 B.C. All of which seems to place the origin of the book of Daniel into the second century B.C.[6]

Persian vocabulary—In an analysis of the Persian words in the book of Daniel, the British scholar Kenneth A. Kitchen noted that the least that can be assumed regarding the date of the book is that it fits somewhere between the sixth to the second centuries B.C.[7]

Kitchen argues that it would be erroneous to suggest that the Persian words took a long time to penetrate into Aramaic. This is particularly evident when one considers the impact Persian had on the Elamite language. Persian vocabulary—especially specialized technical terms and titles from administration, law, and the military—probably drifted quickly into the Aramaic language.

When we keep in mind that after the fall of Babylon Daniel held a high rank in the Persian administrative system, it seems only natural that he acquired many words from his Persian colleagues. It is significant that most of the Persian words found in the book of Daniel designate officials (five of the terms are found in the list of officers cited in Daniel 3:2).

Kitchen further observed that the Persian words in Daniel belong to the period in the history of the Persian language known as "Old Persian."[8] This period came to an end by c. 300 B.C. Kitchen also noted that in the first Greek translation of Daniel (the LXX, which was completed by about 100 B.C.) the translators had already lost the meaning of several of the Persian terms (unless the meanings had changed radically), for their rendition of these words into Greek is mere guesswork.

Had the book of Daniel originated in 164 B.C., as the majority of scholars today argue, only half a century of continuous traditional translation of the book would have passed before the translation into Greek took place. Such a brief interval of time is inadequate, especially by Near Eastern standards, to explain the loss or change of meanings in the Persian words.

The evidence of the Persian vocabulary speaks for an earlier rather than a later date for the book of Daniel.

The Greek words—The three Greek loan words found in the book are all musical terms (Dan. 3:5, 7, 10, 15). They are *kitharis* (from which we get the English words "zither" and "guitar"), *psaltērion* ("harp"), and *symphonia* (often rendered "bagpipe" but literally meaning "accompanying sound").

Kitharis is an ancient word already known from Homer (c. ninth century B.C.). *Psalterion* can be dated to the time of the Greek philosopher Aristotle (384-322 B.C.). Though the word *symphonia* is attested as early as the philosopher Plato (c. 427-c. 347 B.C.) with the meaning of "harmony" or "sounding together," its use as a musical instrument (as in Daniel 3) is so far not documented prior to the second century B.C. The Greek historian Polybius (c. 205-c. 123 B.C.) is the first to mention the term when describing a favorite instrument of Antiochus IV Epiphanes.[9]

It is this second-century date and usage of the word

symphonia that has been crucial for the late dating of the book of Daniel.

In response to this argument, it should be noted that Greek trade in and influence on the Near East go back at least to the eighth century B.C. and therefore could explain the presence of Greek words in the book.

Indeed, scholars who base their second-century date for the book of Daniel on the use of these three Greek loan words seem to be posing the wrong questions. By the Maccabean period the Greek influence in the Near East was so pervasive that in a second-century-origin thesis, the question should not be so much Why are there *three* Greek words in the book? as Why are there *only* three Greek words? During a time of such extensive Greek influence, we would expect a far larger Greek vocabulary and certainly a vocabulary not limited to musical instruments. Once again the evidence tends to suggest an earlier date for the origin of the book.

The date of the Aramaic in Daniel—We have already noted that Daniel wrote his book in two closely related languages—Hebrew (Dan. 1:1-2:4, first part; 8:1-12:13) and Aramaic (Dan. 2:4, last part-7:28). The particular form of Aramaic that Daniel employed has led critical scholars of the past to claim that the book could not have originated in the sixth century B.C. The validity of this charge no longer stands up under close scrutiny.

The history of the Aramaic language has been classified into the following five phases: (1) Old Aramaic (c. 1,000-700 B.C.), (2) Official, or Imperial,

Aramaic (700–300/200 B.C.), (3) Middle Aramaic (300/200 B.C. to A.D. 200), (4) Late Aramaic (A.D. 200-700), and (5) Modern Aramaic.

Until the discovery in the past century of inscriptions in Aramaic dialects, scholars had only the Aramaic of Jewish targums (paraphrases of portions of the Old Testament) for purposes of comparison with the Aramaic of Daniel. Because these targums originated in the Christian era, similarities between these two bodies of material suggested a rather late date for Daniel. This judgment was only slightly modified when, in the middle of the past century, inscriptions in several Aramaic dialects from the Nabatean kingdom (170 B.C. –A.D. 300) and Palmyra (33 B.C.-A.D. 294) were discovered. Because of the even greater similarities between the Aramaic of Daniel and these datable dialects originating in the western ancient Near East, it was concluded that the book of Daniel must also have originated in the west after c. 200 B.C.

This evaluation changed radically since 1906 with the publication of papyri from the island of Elephantine in southern Egypt. The island had been home to a group of Jewish colonists who settled there sometime before the conquest of Egypt by the Persians. The texts from Elephantine threw valuable light on the organization, law, religious beliefs, and practices of the Jews in Egypt during the sixth and particularly the fifth centuries B.C. Detailed examination of these Elephantine papyri revealed that the *Aramaic of Daniel stood closer to that of the Elephantine documents* than to the Aramaic of the targums and dialects.

Though there are some orthographic differences between Daniel (and Ezra) and the Elephantine texts, it has become customary to place them all into the period of Imperial, or Official, Aramaic. Since Imperial Aramaic is placed in the period between the sixth and the third centuries B.C. (a strong case has been made to end this period as early as c. 300 B.C.), the Aramaic of Daniel can no longer be used to argue for the second century B.C. origin of the book.

Additional light has been shed on the dating of Daniel by two Aramaic documents found in Qumran. One of these documents, designated the *Genesis Apocryphon* (1Qap Gen), was published in 1956. On the basis of its ancient form of writing and linguistic grounds, it was dated to the first century B.C. The other, known as the Targum of Job (11Qtg Job), was published in 1971 and placed in the second half of the second century B.C. by its editors. Since both of these works from Qumran differ markedly from the Aramaic of Daniel and require a significant interval of time between their origins and that of Daniel, we have new evidence not only for defending an earlier date for the book of Daniel but also for the unlikelihood of a second-century origin.

The well-known Israeli Aramaicist E. Y. Kutscher and the German Old Testament scholar Klaus Koch have taken the position that on linguistic grounds the Aramaic of Daniel must have had an eastern rather than a western origin.[10] This view further undermines the earlier position that the Aramaic sections of Daniel originated in Judah.

In conclusion, we quote K. Kitchen whose summary has the support of both Kutscher and Koch: "It [i.e., the Aramaic of Daniel] is, in itself, as long and generally agreed, integrally a part of that Imperial Aramaic which gathered impetus from at least the seventh century B.C. and was in full use until c. 300 B.C., thereafter falling away or fossilizing where it was not native and developing new forms and usages where it was the spoken tongue. If proper allowance be made for attested scribal usage in the Biblical Near East (including orthographical and morphological change, both official and unofficial), then there is nothing to decide the date of composition of the Aramaic of Daniel *on the grounds of Aramaic* anywhere between the late sixth and the second centuries B.C. . . . The date of the book of Daniel, in short, cannot be decided upon linguistic grounds alone. It is equally obscurantist to exclude dogmatically a sixth-fifth (or fourth) century date on the one hand, or to hold such a date as mechanically proven on the other, *as far as the Aramaic is concerned.*"[11]

The Silence in Extrabiblical Literature

The absence of references to the book of Daniel in extrabiblical Jewish literature prior to the mid-second century B.C. has been interpreted as evidence that the book did not exist prior to the Maccabean period.[12]

More than 50 years ago Robert D. Wilson responded

to this charge by noting that there are no Hebrew writings extant from before the Maccabean period which could justly have been expected to mention Daniel.[13] An exception is the apocryphal book of Ecclesiasticus (c. 190-180 B.C.), written by Jesus ben Sira of Jerusalem.

Ben Sira gives a catalog of famous Old Testament persons, beginning with Enoch (see chapters 44-50). In chapter 49, where the author refers to Jeremiah, Ezekiel, and the 12 minor prophets, one could reasonably have expected a mention of Daniel. This silence in regard to Daniel is puzzling. However, when we remember that Ecclesiasticus also omits a person as famous as Ezra, it becomes evident that the absence of a name cannot be taken to mean that the person by that name did not exist. No one would doubt the existence of Ezra. Similarly, the argument from silence in regard to Daniel can hardly be taken as proof that Daniel and his book were unknown or did not exist prior to 200 B.C.

The issue before us is not so much a question regarding the existence of Daniel as it is a question about the motive for passing over Daniel's name. Wilson contends that the works of Ben Sira reveal that he was a man of pronounced prejudices and opinions. Although the author does not disclose his reasons for omitting the name of Daniel, a variety of motives, including prejudice, neglect, contempt, etc., could be postulated.

Clearly, Daniel was not unknown in the second century. A reference that rarely receives the attention it deserves, particularly in the context of the charge just mentioned, is found in 1 Maccabees 2:59, 60. Most scholars accept the historical veracity of this passage. According to the author, Mattathias, the father of the famous Maccabees, lay dying. Before his death Mattathias summoned his sons and delivered his final charge. He reminded them of the heroic stand and faithfulness of past biblical heroes. Having mentioned such persons as Abraham, Joseph, Phinehas, and others, he recalled the courage in trial displayed by both Daniel in the lions' den and his three friends in the fiery furnace. With these illustrations the father sought to encourage his sons in their resistance to the tyrant Antiochus Epiphanes.

This event, dated to the mid-second century B.C., reveals that the Maccabean family viewed the stories of Daniel and his companions in the same light as those of other biblical heroes of the past. The dying man would hardly have taken the narratives of Daniel and his fellows as role models in trial had he regarded them to be fictitious. Therefore 1 Maccabees 2 reveals that at least the stories of Daniel 3 and 6 antedate the Maccabean period.

The trend by an increasing number of recent historicocritical scholars to attribute an earlier date to the stories of Daniel 1-6 demonstrates that the argument of alleged silence concerning Daniel cannot be taken too seriously.

Summary

Our analysis, be it of problematical historical issues, linguistic peculiarities, or the argument from silence regarding Daniel prior to the second century, leads us to conclude that a Maccabean date for the book of Daniel falls short of proof. In fact, the information examined so far suggests an early date for the book. Repeatedly we find evidence that the author appears to have had firsthand knowledge of conditions—knowledge that was lost shortly thereafter and only recovered in recent times.

The majority of scholars today concur that the stories of Daniel 1-6 originated in the east and that the Babylonian and Persian empires provided the ideal setting for these chapters.

In the following chapter we will address ourselves to the supposed resemblances between the context of Daniel and Jewish history between 167 and 164 B.C. Do Daniel 11 and related passages in the book reflect the activities of Antiochus IV Epiphanes with such precision that the book's origin (or at least that of chapters 7–12) must be dated in the mid-second century B.C.?

References

[1] Klaus Koch, *Das Buch Daniel* (Darmstadt: Wissenschaftliche Buchgesellschaft, 1980), p. 9.

[2] *Ibid.*

[3] Norman W. Porteous, *Daniel, A Commentary* (Philadelphia, Penn.: Westminster Press, 1965), p. 25.

[4] Raymond P. Dougherty, *Nabonidus and Belshazzar* (New Haven,

Conn.: Yale University Press, 1929), pp. 199-200.

[5] Allan R. Millard, "Daniel 1-6 and History," *The Evangelical Quarterly* 49, No. 2 (1977) : 70.

[6] The classic formulation was given by Samuel R. Driver, *Introduction to the Literature of the Old Testament,* 5th ed. (New York: Meridian Library, 1950), p. 508.

[7] Kenneth A. Kitchen, "The Aramaic of Daniel," in D.J. Wiseman et al., eds., *Notes on Some Problems in the Book of Daniel* (London: Tyndale Press, 1965), p. 37.

[8] *Ibid.,* p. 43.

[9] Polybius, *Histories* 26. 1a. 2; 26. 1. 4.

[10] Cf. Koch, pp. 46, 47.

[11] Kitchen, p. 79.

[12] So again recently in Andre Lacocque, *The Book of Daniel,* trans. David Pellauer (Atlanta, Georgia: John Knox Press, 1979), p. 7.

[13] Robert D. Wilson, "Daniel Not Quoted," *Princeton Theological Review* 20 (1922) : 58.

CHAPTER FOUR

The Maccabean Period; Daniel and Pseudonymity

The Resemblance of Daniel and the Period of Antiochus

Introduction

To modern scholars the most compelling reason for a second century B.C. date for the origin of at least Daniel 7-12 (if not all of the book) is the alleged close correspondence between Daniel (particularly chapter 11) and the historical events leading up to the Maccabean crisis (167-164 B.C.).

John J. Collins writes: "In Daniel 11:29-39 Antiochus' second campaign is described with such precision that it is clearly a *vaticinium ex eventu.*"[1] The description of events Daniel provides,

Collins contends, is so accurate that it must have been penned *after rather than before* the events recorded in Daniel occurred.

According to the Maccabean thesis, the book of Daniel was composed at least in part and/or edited in its final form by an unknown second-century author (or authors) who posed as a sixth-century statesman/prophet by the name of Daniel. This writer, we are told, pretended to have transmitted genuinely inspired predictions about the future (*vaticinia ante eventu*), which in reality were no more than historical narratives in the guise of prophetic predictions (*vaticinia ex eventu*, i.e., prophecies after the event).

The Maccabean thesis, held presently by the majority of biblical scholars, proposes that the actual time when the book was finally composed may be ascertained by (1) recognizing certain identifiable historical hints within the book and (2) by discerning the precise point in time at which the author passed from writing genuine history (the presumption being that Daniel's prophecies are not predictions but past events written up as future predictions) to penning imaginary expectations and mistaken future prophecies. Only a few verses are classified as genuine prophecy (e.g., Dan. 11:40-45). Unfortunately, even these are considered to be mistaken visions of the future.

André Lacocque is typical of most scholars when he writes: "The vision of chapters 10-11 leads us step by step up to the events of 165 (11:39), but before those of 164. The Author knows of the profanation of the

Temple at Jerusalem by Antiochus IV (7 December, 167; see Dan. 11:31). He alludes to the revolt of the Maccabees and the first victories of Judas (166). But he is unaware of the death of Antiochus (autumn 164; see Dan. 11:4ff.) and the purification of the Temple by Judas on 14 December 164. We can at least situate the second part of the book of Daniel (chapters 7-12), therefore, with a very comfortable certainty, in 164 B.C.E."[2]

Once historicocritical scholarship had cut the book of Daniel loose from the moorings of clear biblical statements, it was further compelled to conjecture not only new theories of composition but also of purpose. It is small wonder that questions of composition and purpose have given rise to a "bewildering range of scholarly opinions."[3] This bewildering and at times contradictory range of scholarly opinions does little to inspire confidence in the Maccabean thesis.

While many conservative commentators believe Daniel 8 and 11 predict events between 167 and 164 B.C., they consider these chapters to be sixth-century *predictions* of Antiochus and regard the prophecies as events reaching beyond the tyrant's death down through the period of antichrist on to the end of time.

The critical view, on the other hand, denies not only an early origin of the chapters but also rejects the notion of predictions stretching beyond 164 B.C. Collins states categorically that "it is quite clear that all of Daniel 7-12 is set in the persecution of Antiochus IV Epiphanes (therefore no earlier than 169 B.C.) and at least Daniel

8-12 was written after the profanation of the temple (167)."[4]

Historical Analysis

What then are the historical resemblances between Daniel and the period of Antiochus? Are the similarities so striking that one should ignore the book's explicit claims and accept a second-century origin?

Basic to the Maccabean thesis is the presupposition that a rather reliable historical reconstruction of events between 167 and 164 B.C. is possible and that such a reconstruction coincides so closely with the data provided by Daniel that it could only have been written in the mid-second century. If this proposal is valid and the book arose within earshot of the events of the Antiochian persecution, one would expect a particularly detailed and accurate account of events during this period. Is this the case? In addition, if the putative second-century author was a Maccabean or had Maccabean leanings, as a sizable number of scholars suggest, one would further anticipate seeing some of the significant emphases, concerns, and perspectives of Maccabean literature reflected in Daniel. Can this be demonstrated?

A historical analysis reveals several serious problems with the Maccabean thesis.

First, the most important primary contemporary sources depicting historical events between 167 and 164 B.C. with considerable detail are disappointingly few. They are limited to 1 and 2 Maccabees and Polybius.

Second, several weighty disagreements between these sources about both details and the order of events during the period under discussion complicate matters even further. Events that still remain a matter of controversy among historians include the cause of the religious persecution of the Jews, the precise time of Jason's rebellion, the date of Antiochus' death, and the issue of whether Antiochus conducted one or two campaigns against Jerusalem.

Given the divergences in the presently available primary and contemporary sources, it is difficult to draw up a consistent, detailed, and accurate historical reconstruction for the period under consideration.[5] The problem is compounded by several rather vague allusions in Daniel 11.

All of which highlights the serious difficulty in establishing a satisfactory comparison between the book of Daniel and the mid-second century happenings.

Occasionally scholars will actually use the book of Daniel to round out their historical reconstruction of this period. A case in point is the matter of the two campaigns that Antiochus is supposed to have waged against Jerusalem. Neither book of Maccabees refers to two campaigns by the Greek despot. In view of this difficulty, it is interesting to note the dubious procedure adopted by the well-known Jewish scholar V. Tcherikover. Tcherikover reconstructs events of the period under discussion by considering Daniel 11 (which mentions a twofold contact between the king of the north and God's people) as an eyewitness account of two visits by Antiochus to Jerusalem.

But this process begs the question. Tcherikover assumes what scholars discussing the second-century origin of Daniel are still trying to prove, namely, that Daniel is an eyewitness report of the events under discussion. The validity of this type of circular reasoning is open to question because it is precisely the issue of the two campaigns by Antiochus against Jerusalem that is advanced as one of the major proofs for the second-century B.C. origin of the book of Daniel.

Striking resemblances between Daniel 11 and the account given in the books of Maccabees and Polybius include (1) the reference to the setting up of the "abomination of desolation" (Dan. 8:9-13; 9:27; 11:31; cf. 1 Macc. 1:54); (2) a twofold conflict of the king of the north with the king of the south (Dan. 11:25-29); and (3) the northern tyrant's withdrawal after an encounter with the ships of Kittim (Dan. 11:29, 30). Historians have compared these scriptural details with the profanation of the Jerusalem Temple by Antiochus, his two campaigns against Egypt, and the tyrant's expulsion from Egypt by the Roman consul Gaius Popilius Laenas.

Given this apparent correspondence of events, one can appreciate how people reading Daniel in the time of Antiochus could apply these verses to the situation of their own time. Antiochus left an indelible impression on the minds and lives of the Jews of his day. How could they forget the marches of the Greek army through their territory? Antiochus interfered with their religious observances and ideas. He defiled the Temple by erecting a pagan image on its altar. The hated Greek ruler had attracted traitors to the Jewish cause and persecuted mercilessly those who were unwilling to comply with his program.

Stress on similarities, however, could lead one to pass over the even larger number of dissimilarities and problems. Daniel 8:9-12 and 11:36-39 describe the little horn and the king of the north in terms that far surpass anything we presently know about the actions, character, and pretensions of Antiochus IV Epiphanes.

If our information from extrabiblical sources is correct (e.g., Livy's comment on the religious disposition of Antiochus), then we are left with notable discrepancies regarding the Greek's religious practices and the description in the Bible of the little horn and the king of the north. Consequently, commentators resort occasionally to interpretations dictated not so much by the book of Daniel as by the desire to have the biblical material conform with the information that we have about Antiochus (e.g., comments on Dan. 11:39).

Politically, the reign of Antiochus was far more modest than the descriptions of the little horn and the king of the north given in Daniel 7, 8, and 11. Antiochus inherited the ever lengthening shadow of Rome. When faced with the ultimatum presented by Popilius Laenas, Antiochus, who had formerly been a hostage in Rome, bowed to the superior might of Rome.

If Daniel 7-12 was written shortly after the episodes recorded, as historicocritical scholars contend, why do the biblical accounts reflect so little of the material we read in 1 and 2 Maccabees and Polybius?

Maccabees records a three-year period of temple profanation, but this is not matched by any of the time periods mentioned in Daniel.

If the author of Daniel was a Maccabean or someone sympathetic to the Maccabean cause, one would expect a basic philosophy common both to the books of Daniel and Maccabees. Yet the ethos of 1 and 2 Maccabees and Daniel is at odds. In Daniel there is no call to arms to defend the faith of Israel as there is in 1 Maccabees 2. Daniel is silent about the Maccabean revolt and its leaders. Whereas in the Maccabean literature the freedom fighters and their vicissitudes are of central importance, commentators see no more than a vague allusion to these Jewish soldiers in Daniel (11:34). The book of Daniel is silent about the exploits of the Maccabees and their exciting victories over the Syrian generals. Even if the author had been a pacifist, one would have expected a greater sympathy with the successes of his countrymen. It is hardly likely that such heroes as Mattathias and Judas Maccabeus would have remained unnamed.

The Maccabean letters are concerned with the Jewish *opposition* to this idolatrous king; whereas the book of Daniel focuses primarily on the activities of the little horn and the king of the north.

Proponents of the Maccabean thesis concede that Daniel 11:40-45 does not conform to what is known about the end of Antiochus. Given these discrepancies, commentators claim that the author of Daniel changed from the writing of *history* to a genuine but inaccurate attempt to prophesy. Such an explanation is a *tour de force* that would hardly survive elsewhere in Old Testament analysis. The majority view simply wants to have it both ways and therefore becomes incredible.

If the fulfillment of Daniel 11:1-39 was designed to inspire hope and to validate the fulfillment of future prophecies, then the alleged failure of the events described in verses 40-45 to materialize raises grave questions about the thrust of the total book. The problems would be largely resolved if we were to abandon the Maccabean thesis, recognize Daniel 11 as a genuine prophecy, and seek a different interpretation of the chapter.

In light of these problems, the contention that Daniel (especially chapter 11) parallels events in Palestine between 167 and 164 B.C. so closely that it provides us with the origin of the book needs to be called into question. While the Maccabean thesis demonstrates how those who read Daniel at the time of Antiochus IV Epiphanes could apply sections of this chapter to their own situation, the theory fails to prove that the book (or sections thereof) originated at that time.

Pseudonymity

The Maccabean thesis raises an additional problem. If the book of Daniel was not authored by the sixth century B.C. statesman/prophet who claims to have been the writer of at least portions of the book (e.g., Dan. 7:1, 2), then one has to assume pseudonymous authorship for the book. Yet this slender volume qualified for inclusion in the sacred canon in spite of this alleged pseudonymity. How could this be?

Some scholars suggest that the adoption of the name of an ancient well-known person (a practice that presumably went undetected) was intended to increase the acceptability and authority of the document. Such a practice would seem to border on deception. Other modern writers assure us that attribution of such ancient names to works composed at a later time was an accepted literary practice that deceived no one. Clearly these two functions are mutually exclusive and offensive to the logic and moral sensitivities of nontechnical readers of the book of Daniel.

In the light of Joyce G. Baldwin's observation that during the whole of the Old Testament period "no example has so far come to light of a *pseudepigraphon* which was approved or cherished as an authoritative book," the idea of pseudonymity as applied to the book of Daniel is highly questionable.[6] It robs this biblical book of its very impact.

Gordon Wenham remarks appropriately that "the idea that God declares His future purposes to His servants is at the heart of the book's theology. If, however, Daniel is a second-century work, one of its central themes is discredited, and it could be argued that Daniel ought to be relegated to the Apocrypha and not retain full canonical status as a part of OT Scripture."[7] In any event, the burden of proof that Daniel is in any part pseudonymous still rests with those who make this claim.

Conclusion

The aim of this and the previous chapter has been to examine both the explicit and implicit claims the book of Daniel makes about its composition and origins.

By its own self-witness the book places its birth in the Neo-Babylonian and early Persian periods. Our investigation of the alleged historical problems, linguistic peculiarities, the silence of extrabiblical sources regarding the existence of the book of Daniel, and the proposed correspondence between Daniel and Maccabean history has led us to doubt the claim that these features indicate a late date of origin.

While we are still unable to identify Darius the Mede with absolute certainty and cannot document the professional (and ethnic) use of the term *Chaldean* in Babylonian sixth and fifth century B.C. sources, it is evident that the author of the book of Daniel had remarkable firsthand knowledge of historical conditions in the sixth to fifth centuries B.C.

The presence of Persian loan words and of *only* three Greek terms also suggests an early date. Once we make allowance for morphological and orthographic changes as time passed, we find nothing in the Aramaic chapters of the book of Daniel that precludes an early date. The increase in the number of contemporary scholars who attribute the stories of Daniel 1-6 to the period before Antiochus reveals that the historical and linguistic arguments once used to date the book as late as the second century B.C. presently have less importance.

Likewise, the argument that Daniel (particularly sections of the second half of the book) originated in the second century B.C. because it accurately reflects the Maccabean period is dubious. Contrary to popular opinion, the history of that period is not well known. The main sources disagree on several important issues, and Daniel does not fit this period as well as we have been led to believe.

Although the Maccabean thesis illustrates how people living during the days of the Syrian tyrant's reign could apply portions of the prophecies to their own day, it cannot bear the weight of the argument placed upon it. Much of the detail provided in this slender volume is far better explained when the visions are understood as genuine prophecies (*vaticinia ante eventu*). While one may not want to press for historical correspondences for every detail in a prophecy given centuries before the fulfillment of predicted events, one should be able to expect close parallels in an account that purportedly narrates immediate past events.

In sum, the book of Daniel reflects the background, practices, and customs of the Babylonian and early Persian empires. The author's knowledge of contemporary history and customs, a knowledge lost in subsequent centuries, suggests that the writer lived at the time suggested by the book. Once we accept the validity of predictive prophecy (which is clearly an axiom of faith), there is no reason why the claims of the book of Daniel in regard to its exilic composition cannot be accepted.

The implicit information provided does not contradict the explicit testimony according to which Daniel was responsible for the messages that narrate events in his life and disclose divine forecasts that stretch from the sixth century B.C. to the end of time.

References

[1] John J. Collins, *The Apocalyptic Vision of the Book of Daniel* (Missoula, Mont.: Scholars Press, 1977), p. 8.

[2] Lacocque, *The Book of Daniel,* pp. 7, 8.

[3] John J. Collins, "The Court-Tales in Daniel and the Development of Apocalyptic," *Journal of Biblical Literature* 94, No. 2 (1975) : 218.

[4] Collins, p. 8. More recently J. J. Collins wrote: "Despite the persistent objections of conservatives, the composition of the visions (chaps. 7-12) between the years 167 and 164 B.C. is established beyond reasonable doubt" ("Daniel and His Social World," *Interpretation* 39, No. 2 [1985] : 132).

[5] For a more detailed discussion, see my article "The Book of Daniel and the 'Maccabean Thesis,'" *Andrews University Seminary Studies* 21, No. 2 (1983) : 129-141.

[6] Joyce G. Baldwin, "Is There Pseudonymity in the Old Testament?" *Themelios* 4, No. 1 (1978) : 8.

[7] Gordon J. Wenham, "Daniel: The Basic Issues," *Themelios* 2, No. 2 (1977) : 51.

CHAPTER FIVE

Daniel and Apocalyptic

T heologians generally consider the book of Daniel an apocalypse. What is meant by this designation and how appropriate is it for Daniel? While this chapter will address these questions, the following chapter will explore the implications of our assessment.

Introduction

The study of apocalyptic literature is a recent phenomenon. It began as an independent investigation in 1832 when Friedrich Luckë proposed to examine the book of Revelation (known in the Greek New Testament by the name *Apokalupsis*) in the context of compositions referred to as apocalyptic literature. Though the scholarly inquiry into apocalyptic thinking fell into disuse in the second half of the nineteenth century, it has experienced a revival in theological research since World War II. Regrettably, the subject is extremely complex and has left many questions unanswered.

The word *apokalupsis* is a Greek noun (*apocalyptic* is a derived adjective) meaning "disclosure" or "revelation." The earliest presently known use of the word to designate a literary composition is found in Revelation 1:1. Because the last book of the New Testament is called Apocalypse, it has become customary to designate as apocalypses other literary forms that are similar to the book of Revelation. Apart from John's Apocalypse, theologians generally agree that substantial portions, if not all, of the book of Daniel, and to a lesser degree sections of Isaiah (chaps. 24-27), Ezekiel (chaps. 40-48), Joel (chap. 3), Zechariah (chaps. 9-14), the Synoptic Gospels (Matthew 24; Mark 13; Luke 17; 21), and of the Pauline Letters (e.g., 2 Thessalonians 2), are apocalyptic in nature.

Theologians also label as apocalyptic several documents outside Scripture that resemble the book of Revelation. The more important extrabiblical apocalyptic works of this type include the books of 1 Enoch, 4 Ezra, and 2 Baruch. During the past decade the list of extrabiblical apocalypses has been extended to include not only Jewish and Christian works but also rabbinic,

Gnostic, and pagan Greek, Roman, and Persian writings. In the main, these compositions were generated between the second century B.C. and the second century A.D. in the eastern Mediterranean region.

It is important to remember that by and large historicocritical scholars do not distinguish between biblical and nonbiblical apocalypses. Both the earlier mainly canonical writings and the later noncanonical writings are treated and evaluated by these scholars as if they were of the same cloth. As a result, characteristics alien to biblical apocalypses but typical of nonbiblical apocalypses have been imposed upon the canonical documents. Though there are indisputable and significant likenesses between these two types of works, a failure to distinguish between them has led to a distortion of the biblical compositions, as we will notice. Theologians speak also of "apocalyptic eschatology." This phrase generally designates a perspective characteristic of apocalyptic works, but it is found also in other forms of biblical literature, especially the prophetic writings.

More recently both the noun *apocalypse* and the adjective *apocalyptic* have also been applied as metaphors for our twentieth-century human condition with its crises and agonies. This trend is reflected in articles, books, and motion films that deal with our chaotic and anxiety-ridden age. However, though the fears of our times resemble those described in the ancient apocalypses, we must be careful not to read modern concerns and ideas into the works of antiquity. This is particularly important because, in contrast to those of the past, most contemporary so-called apocalyptic writings are "God-less" and see little hope of a new beginning or any possibility of salvation.

Attempts at Definition

While the word *apocalypse* and its derivatives are widely used, no scholarly consensus has as yet emerged on its precise definition. The reason for this impasse is found in the complexity of the task. Not only are there problems about identifying which books are apocalyptic and which are not; there are also varieties in works presumed to be apocalypses as to literary form, style, date, historical background, and theological outlook.

Before a comprehensive definition of apocalyptic can be attempted, all the works comprising this type of literature will need to be collected. Scholars can then analyze these works and define their characteristics. Unfortunately, this is impossible because only a few documents were originally labeled "apocalypse," and scholars are far from unanimous as to which compositions should be included under the rubric of apocalyptic. Consequently, we need to exercise caution when establishing the limits of the apocalyptic corpus and when attempting to define apocalyptic.

Questions over literary form and theological content further complicate the issue of definition. Confusion is generated when scholars offer definitions based primarily on form or on content rather than on both. In addition, writers tend to concentrate, and understandably so, on that which is distinct and predominant in this type of literature, namely, the dream and vision sections.

At the very outset it should be remembered that the authors of the works we now designate as apocalyptic (including the book of Revelation) did not consider their writings to belong to a clearcut literary category. They simply were not concerned about such fine-spun modern distinctions.

Attempts to express the nature of apocalyptic by simply describing it in terms of a literary form are doomed to failure because the writers of such compositions did not employ a single literary stereotype to express their thoughts. For example, the authors of both Revelation and Daniel communicated their messages by utilizing several literary types, or genres. Even the visions and dreams employ a number of literary forms. At the most elementary literary level Revelation 2, 3 is different from Revelation 12, 13 and Daniel 3-6 varies from Daniel 7-12. To account for this variety and to retain the unity of the works, scholars have proposed recently that apocalyptic literature should be seen as a complex of literary forms with several subforms.

In the past, scholars have suggested both broad and narrow definitions of apocalyptic. Thus the inclination to be inclusive is reflected in the notion that any kind of *revelatory* material, irrespective of content, is apocalyptic. All that matters for this definition is that a composition comes in the form of a revelation. This approach, however, sacrifices the distinctiveness of apocalyptic over and against other types of revelatory material as may be found in classical prophets such as Isaiah, Jeremiah, Amos, Hosea, and others.

On the other hand, theologians, especially those who are inclined to stress theological content, tend to exclude from the apocalyptic corpus works that do not contain previews of history and envisage a cosmic transformation. Accordingly, only those compositions that predict the march of history through time and the cataclysmic change at the end of the world qualify under the rubric *apocalyptic*. This second definition takes its bearings primarily from the visionary materials of the apocalypses but fails to account for such literary features as *hymns*, *epistles*, and *testaments*, which are also found in a book like John's Apocalypse.

A recent attempt to do justice to both manner of revelation and theological content defines *apocalypse* as a kind of "revelatory literature with a narrative framework, in which a revelation is mediated by an otherworldly being to a human recipient, disclosing a transcendent reality which is both temporal insofar as it envisages eschatological salvation, and spatial insofar as it involves another, supernatural world."[1] Though this attempt is more comprehensive and generally quite helpful, it is biased toward a broad definition of apocalyptic.

Given the complexities already mentioned, it is doubtful that scholars will propose a definition which will be generally acceptable. Clearly, then, definitions of apocalyptic literature will have to remain flexible.

Nevertheless, there is basic agreement among theologians about certain literary and theological features that characterize apocalyptic, and to these we now turn. Once we have sketched these features, we can then explore the extent to which the book of Daniel exudes the atmosphere of the apocalyptic writings.

Features Typical of Apocalyptic

The composition originally designated *apocalypse* in antiquity, namely, the Apocalypse of John, identifies itself as a revelation given by God concerning future events (Rev. 1:1). The Greek word *apokalupsis* (meaning "revelation") indicates that the main characteristic of works so designated is their claim to contain disclosures of the future and (as the context of Revelation indicates) revelations of the heavenly realities. In these works the curtain that hides the heavenly world from our view is drawn aside, and we are given a glimpse of the divine world and its involvement in the affairs of our planet.

Revelation 1:1 claims also that the revelation which God gave to John was made known to the seer by an otherworldly being. In contrast to other revelatory literature (such as the prophetic books) in which God predominantly—though not exclusively—gives His messages directly to the human instrument, apocalyptic compositions record messages that in the main have been mediated to the visionary by a third party. The phrase "the word of the Lord," characteristic of the prophetic writings, is hardly ever encountered in apocalyptic. Instead, the figure of an interpreting angel distinguishes apocalyptic works from prophetic literature in general.

Angelic beings are also prominent in apocalypses. Mighty angels speak to or guide John on numerous occasions (Rev. 5:2; 7:1; 8:2; 10:1; 14:6-9; 19:10; etc.). They stand at the four corners of the earth, surround the throne of God, sound trumpets, pour out the bowls of God's wrath, proclaim messages, and minister to John.

Revelation 1:9 informs us that John received the information contained in the book while suffering hardship and persecution in exile on the isle of Patmos. Many apocalypses seem to arise in settings of crisis, despair, and persecution. The messages given John the revelator under such circumstances were to provide instruction, encouragement, and assurance of God's presence and ultimate victory over the present forces of evil (Rev. 1:19).

Striking contrasts (or dualisms as they are called in the theological literature) punctuate apocalyptic works. Thus the book of Revelation draws sharp lines between the seal of God and the mark of the beast (Rev. 7:2; 13:16); the pure woman and the gaudy harlot (Rev. 12:1; 17:1); the armies of heaven and the forces of earth (Rev. 19:11-19); and the new Jerusalem and old Babylon (Rev. 18; 21:2). These contrasts and the distinctions between good and evil, the present and the future, that which is above and that which is below (also evident in other forms of literature), are far more prominent in apocalyptic thought.

Although the prophets and wise men utilized symbols, apocalyptic writing is heavy with imagery. Indeed, the symbolism in apocalyptic compositions is often heightened and composite. Whereas the prophets might refer to ordinary beasts, the apocalyptic author sees a beast with 10 horns and seven heads; it resembles a leopard, but has feet like those of a bear, and a mouth like that of a lion (Rev. 13:1, 2). The One ''like a son of man'' who appeared to the revelator had hair that was ''white like wool,'' eyes like ''blazing fire,'' feet like ''bronze glowing in a furnace,'' a voice like the ''sound of rushing waters,'' and ''out of his mouth came a sharp double-edged sword'' (Rev. 1:12-16).

The visions and dreams of the apocalypses reveal not only the invisible world but also God's long-range plans for human history. Thus Revelation 12-14 describes a series of events that take the reader from the erstwhile conflict in heaven, to the death of Jesus, through ''a time, times and half a time,'' on to the harvest of the earth at the second coming of Christ.

These surveys of history have led scholars to use the term *determinism*, because the time prophecies mediate a knowledge of that which God has *determined* should occur. When referring to apocalyptic literature, theologians do not use the word *determinism* in a philosophical, psychological, or fatalistic sense, implying that God predetermined human choices and behavior. Clearly, human beings may choose to accept or reject God and His kingdom. Rather, the term *determinism* describes the divinely ordained course of events. John J.

Collins correctly notes that "while it is true that no human decision could change the course of events, the fate of the individual was not predetermined. . . . Only the course of the universe and of events is predetermined. These form a framework within which the individual must take his stand."[2]

Generally in apocalyptic writing the unfolding of events is inevitable, and neither human action nor inaction can alter God's plan. We will return to the subject of determinism and explore further its implications in the following chapter.

The features discussed so far are present generally in both biblical and nonbiblical apocalypses. However, it should be added that in later (especially in nonbiblical) apocalyptic compositions we find a much more negative appreciation of history, a greater stress on the imminent end, and an intensification of the dualistic tendencies.

Nonbiblical apocalypses contain two additional elements that we need to discuss briefly. They are pseudonymity and prophecy *ex eventu* (the *vaticinia ex eventu* already mentioned in previous chapters). In order to find acceptance among the people, the authors of noncanonical apocalypses attributed their compositions to the pen of some ancient and well-known sage (e.g., Enoch, Baruch, Ezra). These works also contain depictions of historical events in the form of prophecies. The unsuspecting readers were led to believe that they were dealing with genuine predictions, when in reality they were studying accounts of history merely disguised as prophecy.

Unfortunately, historicocritical scholarship, failing to draw a distinction between the canonical and noncanonical apocalyptic works, imposed the characteristic of pseudonymity and *ex eventu* prophecy upon the biblical works. It seems methodologically questionable that the prophecies of Daniel and Revelation should be treated as pseudonymous works and prophecies *ex eventu* merely because they belong to the category of apocalyptic. After all, the whole purpose of the long-range predictions in the biblical compositions was to affirm the predictive ability and superiority of the God of heaven. Yet the interrelated claims of pseudonymity and *ex eventu* prophecy deny this central message.

Though some of the features just listed are found also in other literary forms of the Bible (e.g., in the wisdom and prophetic books), they *predominate* in apocalyptic materials and taken together set apocalyptic books off from other literary kinds.

Is Daniel an Apocalypse?

Having sketched the typical and recurring features that characterize apocalyptic writings, we may now investigate the extent to which the book of Daniel reflects these elements and thereby evaluate its literary form.

In the book of Daniel the dreams, visions, and auditions take the form of revelations concerning future events. Daniel told Nebuchadnezzar: "There is a God in heaven who reveals mysteries. He has shown King Nebuchadnezzar *what will happen in days to come*"

(Dan. 2:28, NIV). The angel informed Daniel that the vision recorded in chapter 8 "concerns the appointed time of the end. . . . Seal up the vision, for it concerns the distant future" (Dan. 8:19, 26, NIV). In chapter 10 a heavenly being says, "Now I have come to explain to you what will happen to your people in the future, for the vision concerns a time yet to come" (Dan. 10:14, NIV).

Even the stories report dreams and interpretations about the immediate future of Nebuchadnezzar and Belshazzar (chapters 4 and 5). Broadly speaking, then, the book of Daniel comprises a series of revelations that disclose the future down to the time of the end.

Supernatural beings repeatedly mediate and interpret the messages Daniel receives. In Daniel 7 the seer "approached one of those standing there and asked him the true meaning" of all he had seen (verse 16, NIV). In the following chapter the perplexed prophet is once more enlightened by one who stood before him and looked like a man (Dan. 8:15-26). Gabriel returned to give Daniel insight and understanding in chapter 9, verses 22-27. Another heavenly being instructs the prophet in chapters 10-12. While classical prophets usually claim that the "word of the Lord" came to them directly, in Daniel and other apocalyptic works angelic beings mediated between the seer and God.

These heavenly messengers not only conveyed instruction to the prophet but also protected him in the lions' den (Dan. 6:22). Nebuchadnezzar perceived that an angel delivered the Hebrew worthies from death in the fiery furnace (Dan. 3:28). Michael and another heavenly being joined battle with the heavenly rulers of Persia and Greece who were intent on delaying God's purpose for His people (Dan. 10:13-21).

Daniel received his messages while in involuntary exile. Jerusalem and the Temple lay in ruins, and most of the people of Judah were in Babylon. It appeared that pagan foreign nations had triumphed and Israel's God had lost control of affairs. During this time of oppression God gave Daniel visions which assured him and his exiled people that their God was still in command. The divine purpose would ultimately triumph, His people would be vindicated, and the divine kingdom would be established. In a setting of suffering, God's messages gave meaning to the world's agony and provided comfort and hope.

Like the revelator, the prophet Daniel contrasts the kingdoms of this world with the kingdom of God, the little horn power with the manlike being, the persecutor with the persecuted. The seer beholds events occurring in heaven that are contemporaneous with events transpiring on earth (cf. Dan. 7:8-14; 10:12-20). Finally Daniel is assured that present realities will be replaced by future glory (see Dan. 12:8-13). The contrasts are as vivid in Daniel as they are in other apocalypses.

Symbolism abounds in the book of Daniel. We read of a human image, the component parts of which represent kings and kingdoms. A winged lion and leopard, a beast with iron teeth and claws of bronze, a little horn with eyes and a mouth, a ram, a he-goat, a manlike being, are all woven into the tapestry of Daniel's messages. Such composite and vivid imagery is particularly characteristic of apocalyptic compositions.

The surveys of history in Daniel 2, 7, 8, and 11 suggest that God preordained the course of events. Babylon would be followed by Medo-Persia and Greece (Dan. 2:38, 39; 8:20, 21). Other powers would succeed until finally an indestructible and triumphant kingdom of God would totally supersede all human authorities (Dan. 2:44; 7:18, 27). For Daniel, that which "has been *determined* must take place" (Dan. 11:36, NIV).

This cosmic sweep and unfolding of history distinguish Daniel from the classical prophets, whose messages were couched mainly in the conditional language of the covenant. The classical prophets offer occasional glimpses of the distant future but do not unfold the perspectives of history in the manner of the apocalypses. While the classical prophets communicated conditional threats or promises, neither explicit nor implicit conditions are found in the major time lines of Daniel. Although no human decisions can alter the course of events determined by God, individuals remain free to make a decision within the context of God's overall scheme and triumph within the divine plan and purpose.

Reflecting on these features, it becomes obvious that the book of Daniel mirrors the characteristics of biblical apocalyptic. Like the other apocalyptic compositions, the book of Daniel contains revelations of future events and of heavenly realities; its disclosures are mediated by otherworldly figures; its stories and prophecies manifest a particular interest in angelic beings; its origin is found in a time of crisis and its purpose is to provide encouragement; it records striking contrasts; it is profuse with vivid imagery and complex symbols; and it claims that God has predetermined the course of events.

Conclusion

We may now return to our initial inquiry: Is the book of Daniel an apocalypse? Given the complexity of the nature of apocalyptic writings, any answer will require some qualifications. If pseudonymity, prophecy *ex eventu,* and other features of later nonbiblical apocalypses are part of the yardstick of apocalyptic literature, then the book of Daniel fails to qualify. Given the claims of Daniel in regard to date and authorship, the charges of pseudonymity and prophecy *ex eventu* must be rejected.

If we measure the book in terms of the narrow definition of apocalyptic thought referred to above, then only the prophetic chapters can be accommodated under the classification of apocalyptic literature. Although the historical chapters prepare for and anticipate the prophetic chapters, they do not contain forecasts of history, nor do they predict a cataclysmic change at the end of the age.

Given the parameters of the narrow definition, not even the book that gave its name to apocalyptic writings—namely, John's Apocalypse—qualifies as apocalyptic literature in totality. Like the book of Daniel, it includes a variety of literary forms and theological emphases.

Nevertheless, if the book of Daniel is compared with other forms of biblical literature such as wisdom or classical prophecy, then it stands markedly close to the apocalyptic compositions. The apocalyptic nature of Daniel is confirmed by the presence in the book·of the characteristic and recurring apocalyptic features outlined above and its pronounced similarity to John's Apocalypse. On any count, Daniel would be among the earliest works of this type and may have served as a model for this unique body of literature.

References

[1] John J. Collins, "Introduction: Towards the Morphology of a Genre," *Semeia* 14 (1979) : 9.

[2] _____, *The Apocalyptic Vision*, p. 88.

CHAPTER SIX

The Book of Daniel and Historicism

In this final chapter we will explore briefly the implications of the conclusions that we have drawn in the previous chapters. Once we accept the unity, exilic origin, and apocalyptic nature of the book of Daniel, the only consistent method of interpreting the prophetic chapters of Daniel is that suggested by the historicist school.

Historicism (although unfortunately often maligned and caricatured by a variety of highly speculative and contradictory approaches) suggests that the prophetic portions of the book of Daniel take the reader from Daniel's own day, in the sixth to fifth centuries B.C., to the ultimate setting up of God's eternal kingdom at the end of the world (which biblical scholars speak of as the *eschaton*).

The Significance of Unity

In a previous chapter we proposed that an analysis of the structure of the book of Daniel strongly suggests a unity in which the various constituent parts are necessary to the structure as a whole.

The historical chapters introduce us to the main protagonists and record short-term predictions and their fulfillments (e.g., Dan. 4:28-37; 5:13-30). In this sense the earlier chapters anticipate the later chapters. In recording the fulfillment of the predictions concerning Nebuchadnezzar and the fall of the Neo-Babylonian Empire, these early chapters guarantee the fulfillment of the prophecies found in the visions. Fulfillment in the past thus confirms the trustworthiness of future predictions and authenticates the establishment of God's final kingdom. The fortunes of God's people during the Exile become a foil for the experiences of the saints during the period of Gentile dominion.

The total message of the book is ''nothing less than a survey, part historical and part prophetic, of the whole period of Gentile imperial rule from Nebuchadnezzar's first assault upon Jerusalem and the removal of its Davidic king until the abolition of all Gentile imperial power and the setting up of the Messianic kingdom.

Here is no narrow concentration on the few years of Antiochus IV Epiphanes' persecution of the Jews, nor even exclusive attention to the End-time.''[1]

Implications of Exilic Origin

If we accept the claims of the book of Daniel—and we have seen no compelling reason to reject them—then we must accept the prophetic messages as genuine predictions of the future given during the period of the Babylonian exile.

The visions offer surveys of history with a cosmic sweep, and any interpretation that falls short of this sweep must be held suspect. The seer moves steadily and selectively to the establishment of the kingdom of God, when all peoples, nations, and languages will render Him undivided worship and when His saints will receive and possess the kingdom for ever and ever.

As in the New Testament Apocalypse, Daniel's history receives its consummation with the setting up of the kingdom of God. After all earthly dominions are broken to pieces and the saints have experienced both the eschatological woes and the resurrection, the kingdom of God, the end point of Daniel's prophecies, is established.

Modes of interpretation that consider the fulfillment of these chapters to have occurred totally in the past (such as the historicocritical interpretation), or that apply their fulfillment entirely or primarily to the future (such as futurism), or that see in these chapters no more than the eternal confrontation between the forces of good and evil (such as idealism) fail to do justice to the thrust of these chapters. They disregard the repeated temporal indicators that signify *succession* in time, beginning with the Babylonian exile and ending at the eschaton.

Such a sequence in time is indicated by numerical adjectives and words like *after*, *next*, *another*, and others.

Daniel said to Nebuchadnezzar: "*After you, another* kingdom will rise, inferior to yours. Next, a *third* kingdom, one of bronze, will rule over the whole earth. Finally, there will be a *fourth* kingdom" (Dan. 2:39, 40, NIV).

In relating the dream of chapter 7, the prophet saw a *first* animal "like a lion" (verse 4, KJV), then "*another* beast, a *second*, like to a bear" (verse 5, KJV), "*after this . . . another*, like a leopard" (verse 6, KJV), and "*after this . . .* a *fourth* beast" (verse 7, KJV).

Time indicators provide movement in both chapter 8 (e.g., verses 17, 19, 23, 26) and chapter 9 (e.g., verses 24-27).

Temporal terms and phrases like "*three* more kings will appear in Persia, and then a *fourth*" (Dan. 11:2, NIV); "*after* some *years*" (verse 6, NIV); "until the time of the end, for it will still come at the appointed time" (verse 35, NIV); "at the time of the end," (verse 40, NIV); "at that time Michael . . . will arise" (Dan. 12:1, NIV); "until the time of the end" (verse 4, NIV), punctuate the last two chapters of the book of Daniel.

These markers guide the reader like signposts on a journey through time. The path historicism travels does not disappear after a few short footsteps (as the historicocritical interpretation would suggest), nor does it appear out of nothing (as futurism would argue). Rather, it moves in a continuous line, sometimes winding but always forward, beginning with the Exile and ending with the eschaton. This was the understanding of Daniel's prophecies that both the Christian church and Judaism maintained until the recent rise of the Maccabean theory.

The long-range prophecies are replete with symbols that are at times perplexing but not unintelligible. The interpretations provided neither stress nor explain every detail, but they clarify the thrust of the messages.

Thus the manlike image of Daniel 2 represents a succession of empires and rulers beginning with Nebuchadnezzar's empire and ending with God's eternal kingdom. Details such as the precise number of the toes of the image or their precise identity are not highlighted.

Similarly, the imagery of Daniel 7 and 8 is interpreted as signifying kings and kingdoms, but no explanation is given to the significance of the "claws of bronze" or similar details. Evidently it would be presumptuous and probably unproductive—if not counterproductive—for the modern interpreter to advance meanings that have not clearly been revealed. Indeed, it is often these fanciful interpretations that have attracted—sometimes justifiably—the contempt of scholars who have regrettably rejected the historicist approach to the prophecies.

The symbolism of the vision chapters includes time elements that are also cast in figurative language. According to Daniel 7:25, the little horn would oppress the saints of the Most High for "a time, [two] times and half a time." In the audition of Daniel 8, one angel tells another that the sanctuary would be restored after "2,300 evenings and mornings" (verse 14, NIV). What do these somewhat strange time expressions signify?

At the outset, it is important that we recognize the symbolic context in which the temporal expressions occur. Consistency would require that the time elements be treated in the same way as the rest of the imagery.

The interpreting angel clearly said that the ram with the two horns signified the kings of Media and Persia. The he-goat, according to the same interpretation, signified the king of Greece. Consequently, neither the beasts nor the time references should be taken literally. It is most reasonable, therefore, to assume that just as the accompanying images of short-lived animals or parts thereof signified power whose dominion extended over long periods of time, so also the time elements must signify extensive time intervals.

Daniel 9 actually provides a key to the nature and meaning of these expressions of time. The vision of Daniel 9:24-27 begins with a reference to a period of time that literally reads "seventy sevens [or weeks]." The "seventy sevens" commence with the going forth of the decree to restore and to rebuild Jerusalem and continue until the coming of an Anointed, His death, and the destruction of the city and sanctuary.

Both historicocritical and conservative scholars believe that this period must be understood in terms of years to allow sufficient time for the fulfillment of the various aspects specified in verses 24-27. The unfolding of events specified in these verses requires more time than the one year, four months, and several days that a reading of "seventy sevens," or weeks, in terms of days would allow. For this reason commentators and the Revised Standard Version supply the word *years* after "seventy."

This particular interpretation of the "seventy sevens [or weeks]" receives further support from the larger context. Daniel 9:24 takes up both the concept of the seventy years that Jeremiah predicted Israel would spend in Babylon (see Jer. 25:11, 12; 29:10) and the word for "seventy" used in Daniel 9:2. In effect, Daniel says that the time allocated to the events mentioned in Daniel 9:24-27 would be computed by multiplying the seventy years (of which Jeremiah spoke) times seven. The reference to "seventy years" in Daniel 9:2 therefore suggests that the word *seventy* in verse 24 also be understood in terms of years.

In Daniel 10:2, 3 the seer uses the same Hebrew word for "sevens" as occurs in Daniel 9:24. He tells us that he mourned for literally "three sevens of days," or three weeks. On that occasion Daniel modified the term *sevens* with the word *days*.

Commentators, therefore, assume that if Daniel had

meant "seventy sevens of days" in Daniel 9:24, he would have expressed it in the same fashion as in Daniel 10:2, 3, namely, by adding the word *days*. The absence of the modifier *days* in Daniel 9:24 therefore suggests that he intended us to understand the "seventy sevens [or weeks]" in terms of years.

Given the symbolic nature of the time references in the visions, the parallel nature of the visions, and the special link between Daniel 8 and 9, it is not unreasonable to assume with historicist interpreters of past centuries that in the prophetic chapters of Daniel a day represents a year. While the book of Daniel does not state this principle explicitly, Daniel 9:24-27 provides an internal key by which the time prophecies in the remaining chapters may be understood.

Implications of Apocalyptic

In the previous chapter, we mentioned the distinction biblical scholars draw between classical prophecy and apocalyptic but left discussion of the implications of this distinction until now. In what way does such a distinction affect our understanding of the book of Daniel?

Classical prophecy addressed primarily the prophet's contemporaries and challenged them to repentance with covenant promises and threats. Generally, the messages delivered by the prophets were urgent and directed to specific situations. Apocalyptic literature, on the other hand, had the nature of information and instructed the hearers or readers about God's future purposes.

Classical prophecy had its seedbed in the Mosaic covenant—with both its promises and threats (cf. Deut. 27:9-30:20). This theology finds later expression in words such as those recorded by Jeremiah: "If at any time I announce that a nation or kingdom is to be uprooted, torn down and destroyed, and if that nation I warned repents of its evil, then I will relent and not inflict on it the disaster I had planned. And if at another time I announce that a nation or kingdom is to be built up and planted, and if it does evil in my sight and does not obey me, then I will reconsider the good I had intended to do for it" (Jer. 18:7-10, NIV).

The primary aim of the classical prophets, then, was to call their countrymen to decision as they reminded their listeners of God's goodness and stated both promises and threats. In such a context the recipient's response could influence the final outcome. Visions of doom could conceivably be averted by a change of attitude and life. This flexibility of outcome has led scholars to speak of the *conditionality* of much of classical prophecy. Even though the conditions are not always stated, covenantal prophecies exude that spirit. Fulfillment of the predicted results was dependent upon the hearers' obedience or disobedience.

The element of conditionality, so prominent in classical prophecy, is absent from the prophetic chapters of Daniel. There are no conditions given in Daniel 2:28-45; 7:3-27; 8:3-26; 9:24-27; 11:1-12:4. In these visions and interpretations we breathe in an entirely different atmosphere. For Daniel the flow of history is determined by God. The apocalypses convey information that the recipients cannot alter. The fact that the surveys of history stretch far beyond the immediate lifetime of the recipients makes change dependent upon the reactions of Daniel's contemporaries impossible.

Thus the vision of Daniel 8 was given in Belshazzar's third year, which chronologists date to 548/547 B.C., but it envisages the future rise of Medo-Persia (539 B.C.) and of Greece (331 B.C.), to mention only the first elements of this vision. Evidently those living at the time the visions were given had no power either to influence or alter the course of events that God had preordained. From our present vantage point we recognize that history has traveled a path laid out by God, undeterred by the play or counterplay of human affairs.

Commenting on the nature of classical prophecy and apocalyptic writings, John J. Collins observes correctly: "We touch here on a fundamental distinction between prophecy and apocalyptic. The prophetic oracle is addressed directly to the people, calling for decision and repentance. . . . An apocalyptic writing such as Daniel is not communicating a conditional threat. It is interpreting what has already been revealed in cryptic form. Its future predictions have the character of *information* rather than threats or promises. The mysteries contained in either visions, dreams, or writings are already set. Nothing the audience can do will change the course of events. All they can do is understand and adapt to the inevitable.''[2] It is this difference that has led Bible students to speak of the unconditional nature of the apocalypse of Daniel.

To avoid misunderstanding, we repeat that although no human decision could change the course of events, the fate of the individual was not predetermined. The type of determinism we speak of is not absolute. Individuals may hold fast to the covenant or betray it. Since they are open to God's judgment, they must be free to decide. However, individual freedom is exercised within the context of the inevitable unfolding of the course of history.

While there are important similarities between the book of Daniel and other prophetic works such as Isaiah, Jeremiah, Ezekiel, and the 12 minor prophets (e.g., the use of visions, dreams, symbolism, prophecies, etc.), the apocalyptic nature and especially the ''determinism'' of Daniel distinguish it from the prophetic writings generally. The messages of the prophets are predominately conditional (whether the conditions are expressed explicitly or implicitly), but the visions and interpretations of Daniel are unconditional.

An outline of the unconditional and divinely ordained order of events provided people who found themselves in a historical crisis with the assurance that despite apparent setbacks the God of heaven still controlled history. At the end of the day, His purposes would reach their destined goal. As the initial elements of the prophecies were fulfilled and the Neo-Babylonians gave way to the Medes and Persians, the reliability of future predictions was affirmed.

With the passing of time, the prophecies assisted readers of Daniel in ascertaining the distance they had traveled on the path of history. The prophecies continued to assure them of God's constant watchcare and command of affairs. Daniel is certain that absolutely nothing can hinder God's ultimate purpose. In spite of all appearances, the pilgrims are left neither to the fortuitous whims of their fellows nor to the accidental forces of chance.

The God of Daniel is not some absent, unpredictable landlord of the hoary past or distant future; rather, He is Lord of *present* history. Believers can rest assured that God is in control of life *today*. No *human* system holds the key to history or is able to introduce some utopian world government. Ultimately, God overrules and judges in the affairs of men.

Faced by the apparent ambiguity of the unconditional nature and cosmic sweep of Daniel's prophetic visions and the New Testament expectations of the imminent although delayed establishment of God's kingdom, His people had to learn that the infinite God does not measure time in human terms. His purposes know neither haste nor delay. While Christians have been puzzled by the apparent delay of the eschaton for two millennia, Daniel's prophecies have confirmed their conviction about God's foresight and control of history. Fulfillments in the past confirm the reliability of predictions concerning the future and guarantee the setting up of the divine kingdom.

In sum, given the unity, exilic origin, and apocalyptic nature of the book of Daniel, its scope encompasses the history of Gentile dominion, beginning with Nebuchadnezzar's final attack on Jerusalem and ending with the abolition of all Gentile rule when God's kingdom is installed forevermore. The only method of prophetic interpretation that does justice to such a broad conspectus is historicism devoid of the pitfalls of speculation and sensationalism.[3]

References

[1] D. W. Gooding, ''The Literary Structure of the Book of Daniel and Its Implications,'' *Tyndale Bulletin* 32 (1981) : 68.

[2] Collins, *The Apocalyptic Vision*, pp. 75, 76.

[3] For a more extensive recent discussion of historicism, see W. H. Shea, *Selected Studies on Prophetic Interpretation* (Washington, D.C.: Review and Herald Pub. Assn., 1982), vol. 1.